Sandy Willows lives in Mojave with her husband and two young children. Her older children from a first marriage are half grown. She also has a small puppy for companionship.

To my family, children, and friends. The few that palled around when all dealing with similar issues. To my readers in the hope to inspire and relate in dealing with life.

Sandy Willows

REFLECTIONS OF A PRISONER

A BOOK OF POEMS

AUSTIN MACAULEY PUBLISHERS™

LONDON • CAMBRIDGE • NEW YORK • SHARJAH

Ordering Information
Quantity sales: Special discounts are available on quantity purchases by corporations, associations, and others. For details, contact the publisher at the address below.

Publisher's Cataloging-in-Publication data
Willows, Sandy
Reflections of a Prisoner

ISBN 9781647506599 (Paperback)
ISBN 9781647506605 (ePub e-book)

Library of Congress Control Number: 2021918980

www.austinmacauley.com/us

First Published 2021
Austin Macauley Publishers LLC
40 Wall Street, 33rd Floor, Suite 3302
New York, NY 10005
USA

mail-usa@austinmacauley.com
+1 (646) 5125767

Thanks to the staff at Austin Macauley.

Also to those who said:
"Take the risk, you'll never know until you try."

Jail

In this place is hard to see
The things that will come to be.
The walls so cold and bare
Bring about more tears.
Forged friendships to pass the time
And forget about despair.
Food for thought as bread and jam
A coffee break for the lamb.
Release one day in hopes to stay
No more than one last day.
Awaiting freedom's light
And God's hand in its own way.
Love beyond the walls
In hopes we do not fall.

Love

In this tiny cell
Passing time as well
My thoughts wander free
In my dreams you'll be.
Inside my heart forever free.

Kids

You grow as fast as weeds
Faster with each day
Your smiles light up your play
Hugs all the way
Love always come one May.

Sister

Sister oh sister
Why do we fight?
Why do we squabble?
How come you hate
Me more as I wander?
I try my best
You do the rest
This tangled half friendship
We're supposed to share
Nowhere near
Oh sis do you
Say will we ever
Have peace in a day
Tell me how and why
My sister oh my sister.

Longing

This ache is hard
This longing geared
Hope so slim and
shining here.
Peace through tears,
I weep in hopes none hear.
This life astray
The same pain
Another day
Coming so near.

Uncertainty

A long soft silent cry
A life beginning
As it shies inside
A broken heart as it forms
Softly trembling with
Each morn.
Hearing harsh words
Around stumbling and
Looking down.
A painful trial in the womb
Wondering in tune
As words spit forth
From before its birth
A silent cry and shudder
As the night goes by.

Freedom

Will the gates of freedom
Be opened and released
Will there ever be peace.
In this world I'm around
Always looking at the ground.
I long for home and security
Only to be hindered endlessly.
I look to hope in order to fly.
As days and days slowly pass by.
In the midst of seemingly
Chaos entering aimlessly.
Freedom somewhere eternally.

I made two little boys
Grin from ear to ear
Then and there
Now am locked within a tear
Idle nights and long days
Locked inside a cage.
A sin? What to say?
I didn't want this any way.
Let it slowly fade away.

Christmas

By a candle he was born.
His light the stars and
Early morn.
Angels sang his
Sweet lullaby
As his parents
Sat side by side.
Such peace a baby born
To all men
Who mourn.

A Christmas Poem

A starry night
A beautiful moon
Angels singing a
Heavenly tune.
A baby asleep
Upon the hay
A manger where he lay
Animals around they say
As angels stay
Parents along the way.
Indeed it has come
This Christmas day.

Silver

Silver strings
And silver wings
Silver papers and shiny things
Silver stars afar
And silver streaks in the hall
Along the wall.
Silver candles and silver wings
Silver ware and silver beings
Silver moons
Silver spoons
Silver gates in wait
Silver everywhere
I look and see
Silver in someone's hair
Silver anywhere.

Dawn of Another Day

Gray skies and blue skies
I think of two
Full moons and half
I smile at you
Starry nights
And warm lazy days
Sometimes cast away.
Moon beams and sunrays
Some of the best of days.
Lost in thoughts
And away dawn of another day.

Cell Block Addresses

Cell block addresses is what we have.
Tiny rooms behind barred doors.
Sitting, awaiting fate.
Guilty or innocent
Are our pledges and pleas
No contest as can be.
Each day each night
Time for thought
What's wrong and right?
Rethinking things we
Have done, wishing to and o
What's been done.
As we wait the judge tells
Us what awaits
Deciding our fate.

What Is and What's Meant To Be

A silver wall
The sun shining through
Breaks the day brand new.
Tops of buildings and drives.
A bit of hillsides is what we see,
Looking out from this facility
Looking in a window
Through a locked door
Bars and more,
Many locked doors
The views are not the same
But shall we see what is
And what's meant to be.

Brother

Hey brother, what to show
This crazy world we both know
Come visit if you please
Don't ever forget about me.
Do you remember how we played
Chasing dragons away?
A best friend is what we need
Watching out for me.
Your daily grind
My silent time
Hey brother, what to say
Always friends that way
Till we see again the
Light of day.

Sister Somewhat Blue

I know a sister somewhat blue
She had an ache so true
Three boys in clad
Her children through and through,
No girl to rock her world
And make her dreams come true,
All the way through.
So I prayed that God would heed
A gift I wished for two.
A baby girl with ebony curls
And eyes the shade of blue.
In hopes for them I did pursue.
Fleeting true in hopes for two.
In dreams to be happy to,
And mine would come back home to.
A girl for that sister and mister
To bring a smile bright
Her boys and him her delight.
With hopes she'd return
Mine and a friendship
For all time.

Always

Courageous and true
My love does flow
And always know
That part of me is with you
Wherever you may go.
Always as you grow
Softly as the wind blows.

Yellow and Blues

Yellow and blues
Are what they say
Continuously where are they.
No gowns or under-shirts
Beautifully done.
Don't come out less you're one.
Yellow and blues
My uniform
Phyc ward is my dorm.
Each day and night.
Sometimes early morn,
Yellow and blue, what to do.

Prisoners

We are boys and girls
Who grew making bad choices
Through and through.
Some a mistake and others true.
We are here to change and make way
Trying to fight our battles
Day and day.
Some a mistake, a candle
In the wake.
Prisoners are what we are
Our hearts spread so far.
We never know what we get
We tread cautiously upon a stick
Some of us want and long for change
Some of us will stay the same
Guilty or innocent, we see a mistake
Life apart in a work of art
Another chance we hope to start
Everything depends upon
What's in our heart.

Each day I shift
Each day I miss
Each life apart
Nowhere bliss.
A can of worms
A manic dorm
A steadfast uniform
Outside seems far.
I like the door ajar
Locked inside a pen
My only choices to fit in.
Each night I wait
Sleep a lowly escape,
When awake I tend to pace!
My family, what to do
Oh how I miss you.
Each smile of hope
Fear taking the rope.
A slight hope
One day to return
No longer in a dorm
Fighting a stressful storm
Home again by the morn.

What to think.
What to say
I love you anyway.
Locked away inside the halls
A maze of doors and
Chambers near.
When can home become so dear?
I miss the sun, the warm winds blow
Ready and waiting to be let go.
Faces and smiles in my dreams
Too far away to be seen.
Locked away, what to say
Dreams take me far away
Nights are low
Days are slow
Home someplace I long to go.

Past and Present Meet

Counting back what to say?
Eighteen years today
A family lighted my way.
Three boys so true
Three happy girls too
All with eyes of blue.
My life apart
Seems tart
It's about time to start.
One family, one home
Maybe a garden gnome.
The parents did part
Another start.

A family through and through.
Many thoughts of you.
The latest edition now due.
One day seems true.

Deputies

We are men and woman
Of the shield
We work so hard in the field.
Protect and serve is what we do.
You break the law we'll
Come after you.
Inside you will be
For a time you shall see.
No double deals
Or silent thrills,
Much less our spills.
We try to be fair
As we dare.
Remember, we can stare.
Once inside, we can hide.
To stay outside
Please abide
Don't break the law
And you shall see
We are people
As to be
Our jobs is what

We must do
Mind the laws
To be free
Inside is not
The place you want to be.
We are the deputies.

Walking amongst these halls
I call out in despair
Wondering who really cares.
A friendship deep within
Slowly entering in.
A peace to a tormented soul
Trapped in a hole.
Looking around I look in
Jesus you're slowly becoming
My best friend
Please be here till the end.

Release

The gates opened wide
As they led me down the hall
In chains, walking against the wall
Nods here and there in hopes
To not return
A hard long lesson learned
A promise to a cop
As they walked me along.
Freedom steps away
Releasing me that day.
The wind was cool upon my face
A new breath of life in place
Arms if a few opened wide
As I turned to say my goodbyes
No longer locked inside
A cell like hell
Fixing my life is where I dwell
Release for me and the little
One inside time now slowly goes by
I'm reaching the point of no return
My backs been stabbed
Broke, bruised, and worn.

My heart laid upon the floor
As love slowly walks out the door
I try my best in evening's rest
To forget to seize to make-believe.
A showered might I try to find
A mended body and mind.
Issues rear their head
As I am slowly led
One step ahead two more behind
Racing in my mind
Life's highways and bi-ways
Fold and unwind
A check behind.
The past haunts me
Across my mind
My life unsure as I slowly climb.
These ropes, these ladders
And hidden scopes
A downhill and uphill slope
A cloak upon my back
Awaiting another slap
Then cautiousness cuts in
Telling me begin again
Each day passes along the share
I can hardly take it anymore
Troubles I want to forget
Then again I slowly slip
A day of happiness equipped
I try to find as I walk along a line.

Why Smile

Why smile, when you're down
Waiting for people to come around?
Why smile when your life
Is a simple stain upon the ground?
Why smile when you're torn apart?
Why smile when your heart
Is refusing to start?
Why smile when you're away
Waiting cautiously for another day?
Why smile at all
So you can tell people
You're not going fall?
Why smile for a while
To show your faith
Has not called or crawled
To hide your pain
In the raw,
As well as your flaws?

What do you do?
When life has gotten you down
When the spark has worn down
When time has gotten you on the ground.
When love seems vague
When happiness is changed
When things seem to turn
And life has caught you in a storm
What do you do?
Ask another above to
Love you through and through.

Untitled

Locked inside a room
Wings broken and blue
Staring through the glass
As I face my past
Taking flight upon
Evenings light
A cascade of feelings
Crushing through
My heart losing blood
Deep inside of me
Prayers fleeting desperately
As I journey back to me
Dark abyss of nothingness
Shields my eyes
So I can't see
What to do
That brings pleasantry
Each whisper a note
A flittering nope
Slumber some
Peace to a tormented
Soul who has lost control.

Moving on

I could be someone's
Cheerleader if given a chance
I could be a fantasy as we dance
I could do my best to be true
But first I must get over you
Each step I take for me
Sometimes brings me glee
Then it's tossed back to me
I could be a one and only
If you could only see
How much you mean to me
For this time now is free
Just joining like a bee
Waiting is hard for me
So I need to set free
Life now begins with me
For now it's best to let you be.

My Everyday Hug I Need

The warm water cascades down
Wiping some stress away
A self-hug I need everyday
My life somewhat empty
And incomplete my heart
A train wreck as I lay down
To sleep
Injustice has been done
Living my life in my mind
On the run
Accepting what's been done.
One day an angel
Asked God what was wrong?
He said my child is so unhappy
I give her love I hear
Her prayers but in the
End she wishes I was there
I try my best to show
I'm there but in her
Darkness he draws near
She asks me how to live
She asks me if I really care

Her eyes are sad
And filled with tears
Her heart is whole
And wistful and true
But she cannot believe
The words I love you
She wishes she could leave
The earth and travel
Spiritually and free
A lot of times she blames me.
She wants to roam
With angels an unseen entity
She prays to be set
Free and deep inside
Her heart she wonders
About me.
I've learned she is not
The only one but I
Cannot be the pain
She feels ranges
From me
So I look at her in my hand
And whisper someday
You'll understand
Till then know it's not me
The bad things quickly
It's not me but an
Attack please don't turn
Your back
Know deep inside the light
Shine eternally be patient

And what is meant to be
Will be.

Thinking on the Past

I know it's hard I've been
There to don't ever think
My thoughts never wonder
Of you.
Trials make you strong
Even when things go wrong
Know I'm there for
You and always care
All you need to do is
Say I'm trying for
Another day.

Forgot about God Today

I forgot about God today
For a minute or two
Then remembered how
Much He cares
And how much He holds dear
To Him
How much He suffered
Despite our ignorance
I forgot for a minute
All I have is Him
I forgot without Him
I will not win
I missed Him and
Cried remembering
How He died
Then I remembered
Unto Him my hopes
And fears and dreams
And my despairs
Knowing He knew
Even though I'm blue
Then I remembered

He loves Me just
For being me
My God eternally
A mixed-up, flawed
Human being He
Made perfectly
One of many on
This earth from
Since our birth
To this day
In many a ways
Trying as we may
I've been so angry
This is true my thoughts
Of love turning blue
I try so hard
Just to pay
I argue with God
Every day in every way.
I try my best
To block out thoughts
Of you
My face turning red
As I bite my tongue
On things I want to say
Trying to understand
How things went this
Way, trying hard to live
Another day.
Then I remember you
A world turned against

And still say I
Love you all in every way
Each and every day
Then I began to pray.

Ignore

I can't talk to you
Anymore my life is a
Locked door.
I can't visit no more
Because all you do is ignore
Positive thoughts try to
Enter met with negativity
All around.
Why prove myself or try
When you just pass
Me by.
Why hope when all you
Do is choke why care
When all you do is stare.
Why laugh when things
Are funny when all I
Am is mocked.
My life, my hope, my rope
Cut off at the top.
Abandoned and left
To rot.
Dreams crushed in naught

So life I do revoke
When freedom is on the choke.
Free to love, to live, to
Get by I would not
Pass by.
But every hope or thought
Straight up mocked.
As you doubt and disbelief
Wish me ill will instead
Harmony. The truth sought
Out to be free. There is
Hardly anything left of me
But a shell of what
I used to be.

Searching the Window of Life

Is there a life someplace else
For my children and me
Where a ghost is a person
Instead of in my head
Uncondemned for being me
An occasional drink without
Being tipsy
Where I can be me and
You can be you without
The looked down upon
Or worse these things
They say play in
And with my head and heart.
Where we can be what
We are meant to be,
And these things will not
Bother me, us or them,
Even slightly him.
Especially me and them.
Because my wings
Seem too short to fly
These days bye and bye.

Voices

Oh what can this be
These things I fight
And see, hearing as
They whisper to me.
Each time I try to mend
In thought, heart, and mind
They surround me.
What shall I say
Into each day.
Think, retreat, resent,
Or make since.
What does it mean
To control when others
Naught to this day
Were taught.
Each daybreak and
Evening's dusk.
I look toward the
North and then to
The South and often
More than not the
East I know for sure.

Should I look toward
The West or wait
And grieve some more.
They say you're gone
They say don't stay
They say let go
In every way.
Just don't lose
Control of self
And circumstance
What can this be
And why to me.

If I Wrote a Book on My Life

If I wrote a book
On my life it would
Be a tale of something
Between heaven and hell
It would tell about my life
In more than one way.
As I struggled to
Get to paradise, day by day.
It would tell and contain
Trial and error, ups and
Downs, and ins and outs.
Some good times and a lot
Of bad times.
Include success and failures
Time and time again
Things from fitting in
To dreams and fantasies.
Waking up to reality.
To this day I said no more.
My heart aches no longer
Numbered any more, and galore.
To the point of exhaustion

And the struggle of
Defining me.
With hopes of success
Finally in more than
One way.
Up until the point
Of my dying day.
It would be a daring tell.
Of horrific battles and white nights
Wins and losses and
Graphic to from childhood to more
With monsters and
The one who paid
The price.

Pieces

Pieces of my life
Jumbled inside my
Head. Sorting through
One step at a time
Going what's it mean to you.
The day you left
I was blue.
These thoughts all askew.
Inside, outside, what if,
Any can I get through.
One try at a time.
I'm going, I'm way behind.
What to do?
This way, that way
I came unglued.
Some things said
Others done.
What happened to you?
I know what happened
To me I got screwed
And ready to punch you.

Good Morning Sunshine

Good morning, good sunshine
Good morning, moonshine
Hello day, want to play?
Mmm… lunch time it's afternoon.
Good night, nighttime
Go away, monster
I'm here to stay
And what do you know
There's the moon.

Teardrops

One teardrop here
Two teardrops there
When the raindrops fall
Here they come down my eyes
One for a friend
Two for a love
Three for the one that
Turned away.
Try and try again.
I want to say goodbye
And keep a thought in
My heart.
Which has dwindled to
A tiny spark.
Keep trying a soft whisper
In my ear.
Surges the spark to the
Flame within my heart
How to escape the dark
One way or another

What can it be?
I want to leave and surge
Be free.

My Guardian

I have a guardian
Angel his hair is
Reddish brown.
I have a guard dog
Who follows me around
And he is jet black.
I have a crazy gringo
Always chewing out my ass.
I have a sister who sits back
I have a friend somewhere
His hair is black.
I have a funny little
Friend who makes
Me laugh.
I have a brother
Who hopes things
Come to pass.
I have six little
Hearts that ask
For me each day.

And an angry temper
Who tells me to go away
Then begs me to stay.

Dreaming

Sitting in the desert sun
Pondering what's been done.
My wild friends wander by
And say hi.
Rocky the raven sits atop
A pole squawking and
Cawing his hello,
Hansel and Gretel wander
Through the yard the
Feathers on their head held high.
Loner the turtle dove pauses
From his day doing from
His post along the way.
Peter my wild,
Bunny friend, hops along his
Way munching on grass
And veggies tossed his
Way, as well as bushes on
The way.
Scooter, the hummingbird,
Flitters and plays
Hovering for breakfast

Come his way.
Resting on a branch
To watch me on the day.
Woody and Wendy the
Woodpeckers visited
One day to search for
Bugs in wooden poles
And trees going and
Coming as they please.
Blue boy the mountain jay
Comes and goes away.

Annie the ant lion awaits
To dine in her hole
By the pine.
Timothy the rat his
Family is too big scurries
Along the walls as the
Night begins, beg him
To live in the desert
With the coming wind.
The little house finishes
And sparrows dart around
Taking a sip or a bath
As the sprinkler goes
Around.
These wild animals I
See wishing to understand
Them in a way.
Just to hear some
Say why have you
Named them as they
Play and wander
Free, and visit the
Yard this day.
Troubles the squirrel

Romps and plays
I watch from afar
As I sit staring
At the stars.
Relaxing during
The day, nature
I do respect from
Afar. As I search
My own answers near and far.

Curiosity

Your touch wanders across
my body. Your stare
penetrates my soul
life and longing made
whole
I close upon a shadow
Of debating self-control.
My body trembles and
Aches as you wander to
And fro
I try to make sense
Of sensations beyond control
Your words locked away
In my soul.
Try as I may losing
Control.
Your kiss softens my glare
Silence coming near
Try as I might
The fight has let go.
A question of is this
The way to go.

Homeless

The wind tussles
With my hair, as thorns
Sink into my shoes,
The desert sun blisters
My skin as the day
Breaks in.
My coat is torn my blanket
Worn, a building or tree
My only dorm.
The stars are my night
Lights as the moon
Shines bright
These roads I walk
And wander free
Lost in thoughts of
My own curiosity.
My only friend
The shadow at my side
Conversations that
Sneak out and by.
My past a sea
Of forgiveness my

Glass a faded
Bottled dish.
What am I as I go by
The homeless of this
Land do you dare
Take my hand
In my frightful
Disarray the
Appearance of
My former days.
Choices I have made
Good or bad what it
May.
My solemn lonely days.

Christmas Wish

A home to call my own
A bed to rest my head.
My children gathered round.
A present beneath the tree.
Peace eternally.
Good food to share
In pleasant company
Christmas carols playing
Upon the stereo
Bright lights and bows.
Icicles and mistletoe.
Wars to end
And families on the mend.
And new dreams
To begin
Blessings from above.
Good tidings for all in need
A simple wish
From beneath the tree.
Family, friends, and me.
Chatting happily.

It's Time to Say Thanks

Thank you for the bed
Where I lay to rest my head
Thank you for the food
Upon my little table
Thank you for the clothes
That cover my back.
Thank you for the shoes
Upon my feet the
Blessing of new friends
Thank you for tiny smiles
On bad days that make
Me laugh and play
Thank you for company
Little visits or stays
Thank you for my life
In every way.
Family gathered round
As we pray talk
And say, and children
Play.
Thank you in every way
Thank you for the trials

That make us strong
The struggles when
We do wrong
Thank you for your
Life for you are
The one who paid.
The ultimate price.
To live free
And search the sky eternally.

One Wish

One wish to have
One wish to keep
One wish for something
Deep.
One wish to wait
One wish to state
One wish to please and
Be free.
One wish for things
Eternally
One wish to try
As days go by
One wish to leave
Pieces of me.
One wish I hope
One wish to float
One wish to be
Set free.

Untitled

My heart a bit asunder
My life of plunder
My anger shows its
Might deep within
Evening light… my dreams
A scatter across the land
My pain showing in my
Hand. My hope above the
Days deep in dreaming
Delight…my life a bit
I wonder my hope sagging
But not lagging my show
Of faith in what I do…
I love you … I may not be
The perfect one but I
Know I will try … my life
Unending my pain mending
My love shining bright
As the sun breaks
The light.

New year

The new year
Has come to pass
A new start you
Hope lasts.
A wish for things
To change joy
And no pain.
A hope anew for
Good things through
And through.
A place at your
Own is what you
Need to do
A hope spring
New no promises
Or demands
As long as
You're in command.
A place of
Peace just
For you
Second chances

A few.
A new slate
To begin in
Hopes of
Good things
Coming through
A new year
To do and get
Through.

CPSIA information can be obtained
at www.ICGtesting.com
Printed in the USA
BVHW081221111121
621212BV00010B/1145